You Might Be A Football Fan If . . .
Simplified Game Notes for Would-be Fans

Dorothy D. France
with Jason and David Frankle
Cover design and illustrations by John Cooper

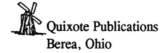
Quixote Publications
Berea, Ohio

Copyright © 2000   Printed in the United States of America.
by Dorothy D. France   All rights reserved.
with Jason A. Frankle and David A. Frankle
Illustrations © 2000 by John Cooper

Quixote Publications   First edition   10 9 8 7 6 5 4 3 2 1
490 Merrimak Drive   ISBN 0-9677583-8-6
Berea, Ohio 44017-2241

Playing field diagram reprinted with permission of the National Federation of
State High School Associations. Officials signals reprinted with permission of
the National Collegiate Athletic Association.

                    Library of Congress Cataloging-in-Publication Data
France, Dorothy D.
  You might be a football fan if--: simplified game notes for would-be fans / Dorothy D.
  France with Jason A. Frankle and David A. Frankle ; illustrations by John Cooper.--1st ed.
    p. cm.
  Includes index.
  ISBN 0-9677583-8-6 (alk. paper)
    1. Football--United States--Terminology. 2. Football--United States--Miscellanea. I.
  Frankle, Jason A., 1980- II. Frankle, David A., 1982- III. title.
GV950.6 .F72 2000
796.332--dc21   00-035282

To the 1998–1999 and 1999–2000 Indians

Copley (Ohio) High School

Regional Semifinalists and Finalists

Coaches and Players

Parents and Fans

Contents

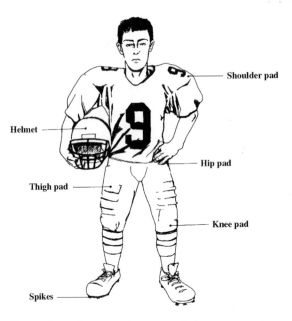

Shoulder pad

Helmet

Hip pad

Thigh pad

Knee pad

Spikes

Special equipment is needed for protection.

Foreword

As a football coach, I believe very strongly in the value of football. It transcends social strata and allows individuals to become a team, a community, a family! It is a game played within a set of rules and boundaries, but its effects have no limits. It is a game of passion, brute force and dignified beauty. Football touches both young and old, in every region in America, played by 80-pound peewees and by 300-pound-plus behemoths. It is a game that is constantly teaching lessons.

I would like to thank Dorothy, Jason and David for this informative book. I am sure that it will enable many more to enjoy the beauty of the game of football.

Dan Boarman
Head Coach
Copley (OH) High School

Introduction

Have you ever been a spectator at a ball game, cheered along with everyone else, and then turned to your friend or the person behind you and asked, "What just happened? I thought we had the ball."

Well, I have. I did it so often at my grandsons' football games that I decided that even after watching and attending games for years, I still didn't know the rules. So I made the rounds of the bookstores to find just the right book. I didn't find it. They were all too complicated for me at my age.

Even the picture books that I could understand a little didn't include any information on the unwritten rules—those little extra happenings before the game, on the sidelines or in between plays. So I began to ask my grandsons *too* many questions and would get an answer or two now and then. Finally, I said, "Why don't we write a book together for people like me and other would-be fans?"

This little book is the result of that question.

The real understanding of the game came not after I began to understand the rules and what was happening when the ball was in play but when I began to understand what was taking place in all those times in between.

• The team comes on the field, begins to form a huddle, the players pile on with the last person making a running leap onto the top. That's called "getting the players and fans fired up."

• The warm-up period is nearly over, and you see one or more players come off the field, kneel on the sidelines, and the trainer does something to the helmet. That's called "making the helmet fit properly" by pumping air into it. You don't dare call the players "airheads" however.

• During the game, particularly when the weather is hot and players are substituted in and out of play or when time out is called, the water boy hastens to provide the bottled water. There seems to be an unwritten ritual with that bottle: you grab it, take a sip and spit it out; take another sip and spit it out. Then you pour some on the top of your head, and the rest goes down your back. That's called "cooling off."

• After a good play, teammates on the sidelines may bump their helmets together as if they are getting ready for a bullfight, but that really means "We did it" or "That was great."

• A rough play takes place as players defend or block other players. Shoulder pads hit with a loud thump. Don't worry. That's a good sign. That sound means the pads have kept the players from getting hurt.

• Making a good play may ensure that you'll get a lot of whacks on the head by your teammates. That's not a sign of anger but translates, "Good job," "Way to go" or "Do it again."

• A player comes off the field and goes to the trainer who sprays his jersey with something from a bottle. It is not exactly "spray and wash," but the solution does remove the blood and thus any contamination that could occur. At one game Jason came to the sidelines with blood on his shirt and hand. As he was being sprayed, he looked up at me and yelled, "Don't worry, NaNa. It's not my blood. It belongs to the other fellow."

And so it goes.

Football is a great way to share with family and friends, and it builds community.

D.D.F.

GETTING STARTED

Basic information you should know

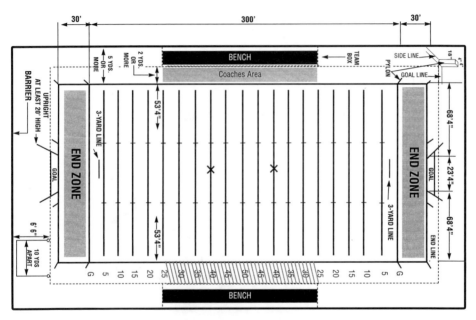

The Playing Field

16

You might be
a football fan if . . .

You know that

you can watch the game alone, but

you cannot play the game

alone.

Football is a team sport. In addition to the players, there are coaches, trainers, officials, cheerleaders, moms, dads, grandparents, loyal fans and opponents.

You might be
a football fan if . . .

You know that

neither snow, nor sleet, nor fear

of frostbite will cause the

game to be canceled.

The game is played outdoors on a field that is 120 yards long and 53.33 yards wide; the playing part of the field is 100 yards long, and each end zone is 10 yards deep.

You might be
a football fan if . . .

You know that

the excitement and anticipation begin

when the players first arrive

on the field.

The game officially begins with the kickoff and ends after 48 minutes of play, unless the score is tied and the game goes into overtime. The game time is divided into halves and the halves into quarters. Each half is started with a kickoff.

You might be
a football fan if . . .

You know that

the **COIN TOSS** determines

which team kicks off first.

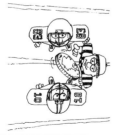

Before the scheduled game starting time, the referee, in the presence of the field captains, tosses a coin, which the visiting captain calls. The winner of the coin toss chooses whether to kick or receive or to defer his team's choice to the second half.

You might be
a football fan if . . .

You know that

being able to count to eleven

is sometimes a challenge.

Each team shall begin the game with 11 players, but if it has no substitutes to replace injured or disqualified players, a high school team may continue with fewer. However, when on offense, a team must have at least seven players on the line of scrimmage.

You might be
a football fan if . . .

You know that

a player is in trouble if he throws

the ball and it comes back

like a boomerang.

The object of the game is for one team to carry or pass the ball across the opponent's goal line or to kick the ball through the opponent's goal by a placekick or dropkick. The team scoring the most points at the end of the game is the winner.

You might be
a football fan if . . .

You know that
players have to be ready and
willing to take a hit.

Players wear special equipment to protect themselves from receiving injuries. Each team has trainers on the sidelines to assist players in case of injuries or equipment problems.

You might be a football fan if . . .

You know that

the men in striped shirts have not

just pulled off a jailbreak.

The officials—judges, umpires, referees—make judgments and decisions to enforce the rules of the game and call the penalties. They use whistles, chains, yellow flags and small sandbags to help them to monitor the plays as the game progresses. Their decisions cannot be appealed.

You might be
a football fan if . . .

You know that
some cheerleaders and fans may not
always know who has the ball,
but they keep on
cheering.

Cheerleaders and fans play an important role in boosting morale and keeping spirits high. The cheerleaders are carefully chosen through tryouts, and the fans display their enthusiasm and support for their special teams.

You might be
a football fan if . . .

You know that

the band and halftime go together like

football and hot dogs,

green eggs and ham or

peanut butter

and jelly.

During the intermission at halftime, the bands march onto the field to show school spirit and support for their teams; the players go to the locker room for the coach's words of wisdom, and the Booster Club welcomes the fans to the concession stand.

You might be
a football fan if . . .

You know that
coaches, players and officials
speak and understand
"pigskin" language.

Terms like *backfield in motion, bump and run, dead ball, forward pass, Hail Mary, curl pattern, pocket* and *spike* can be confusing if you are new to the sport.

PLAYING THE GAME

Terms to help you follow the game

You might be
a football fan if . . .

You know that

AUDIBLE is not the way to

share your personal secrets.

Audible is what a quarterback does from the line of scrimmage when he changes the play from what was given in the huddle by calling out new signals to his teammates.

You might be
a football fan if . . .

You know that

the **BALL CARRIER** is not

the lead seal

in a circus act.

A ball carrier is any player who has possession of the football.

You might be
a football fan if . . .

You know that

a **BLOCKER** is not the one who

lays bricks at a construction site.

A blocker is a player who uses his body to prevent an opponent, a defensive player, from getting to the ball carrier. He can block with his arms and body but may not hold an opponent.

You might be
a football fan if . . .

You know that

BUMP AND RUN is not one of the
rules posted at the entrance to
the bumper cars at the
fair.

Bump and run is a technique that the defensive back uses when he bumps the potential pass receiver to slow his progress at the line of scrimmage and then runs down the field with the receiver.

You might be
a football fan if . . .

You know that

the **CENTER** is not the filling in a

Tootsie Roll pop.

The center is the offensive player who starts each play by snapping the ball to the quarterback.

You might be
a football fan if . . .

You know that

CHAINS are not the ones worn by
prisoners when they clean up
the highway.

A 10-yard length of chain is used to measure the distance required for a first down. The play is stopped and the sideline officials walk in with the chains and measure to see if the offensive team has advanced the ball the 10 yards needed for a first down.

You might be
a football fan if . . .

You know that

a **COUNT** is not the title

for a French nobleman.

The numbers that a quarterback shouts before snapping the ball are known as the count. He has informed his teammates in the huddle that the ball will be snapped on a certain count.

You might be
a football fan if . . .

You know that

a **CURL PATTERN** is not

done by a hair stylist.

Curl is a pattern an offensive receiver runs in anticipation of receiving a forward pass from the quarterback.

You might be
a football fan if . . .

You know that

a **DEAD BALL** is not the one

just flattened by the

stadium crew.

The ball is dead when a play is over and is live as soon as it is legally snapped or free kicked and a down is in progress.

You might be
a football fan if . . .

You know that

DOWN is not the goose feathers

used to stuff pillows

or ski jackets.

A down is one of four chances a team on offense has to gain 10 yards. It also refers to the state of a player who has just been tackled.

You might be
a football fan if . . .

You know that

the **END ZONE** is not

to be confused with

tunnel vision or

a dead-end street.

End zone is an area 10 yards beyond each end of the playing field. To score, a player must get into the end zone or kick a field goal. Each team defends one end zone.

You might be
a football fan if . . .

You know that

a **FAIR CATCH** is not what happens

when a guy steals his

best friend's main squeeze.

The receiver of a kick signals for a fair catch by raising one arm directly above his head. He then is protected against being tackled when he makes the catch but gives up his right to advance the ball.

You might be
a football fan if . . .

You know that

FIRST DOWN is not a game that

little children are willing

to play at bedtime.

A first down is the first of four chances that a team on offense has to advance 10 yards down the field. As soon as a team gains those yards, it earns a new first down.

You might be a football fan if . . .

You know that

a **FLAG PATTERN** is not made up

of the stars and stripes

blowing in the wind.

Flag pattern is a pattern an offensive receiver runs while trying to receive a forward pass from the quarterback. The receiver runs 10 yards, then angles his course toward the corner of the end zone.

You might be a football fan if . . .

You know that

a **FORWARD PASS** is not a

move made in the front seat

of a car.

A forward pass is a pass thrown on a scrimmage play toward the opponent's goal line. Only the offensive team may throw a forward pass. It must be thrown from behind the line of scrimmage.

You might be
a football fan if . . .

You know that

a **FULL HOUSE** is not a poker hand.

Full house is an offensive set where all the running backs are behind the offensive line. There are no split receivers.

You might be
a football fan if . . .

You know that

FUMBLE is not what a lover wants
to do when proposing to
his girlfriend.

A fumble takes place when a player carrying the ball loses possession of the ball by dropping it. If it is recovered by the defense, they now have possession of the ball.

You might be
a football fan if . . .

You know that

a **GIRDLE** is not the kind to

shop for at Victoria's Secret.

The girdle is similar to a pair of shorts and holds protective pads.

You might be
a football fan if . . .

You know that

GOING FOR IT is not what's done at
an all-you-can-eat buffet.

Going for it occurs when a player facing a fourth down decides to try for a first down instead of punting. If the attempt fails, the team loses possession of the ball.

You might be
a football fan if . . .

You know that

a HAIL MARY is not a way

to make amends after

committing a sin.

A Hail Mary is a long pass thrown toward the end zone (goal line) with the hope that a teammate will catch the ball and score.

You might be
a football fan if . . .

You know that

a **HANDOFF** is not what grandparents
do with their grandkids
after they have spoiled
them rotten.

A handoff is a running play in which the quarterback hands the ball to a running back.

You might be
a football fan if . . .

You know that

HASH MARKS are not the ones worn

on a uniform to show years

of service.

Hash marks are the inbounds line markers, spaced one yard apart, that fix the point where the ball is put into play. Each play must begin on or between the hash marks.

You might be
a football fan if . . .

You know that

HOME FIELD ADVANTAGE is not

the farmer's easy access

to his cornfield.

Home field advantage is the benefit a team gets by playing games in its own geographic area. Plus facttors are fan support, familiarity with the field and the lack of required travel.

You might be
a football fan if . . .

You know that

a **HUDDLE** is not what happens

when a person

wants to be alone.

A huddle takes place when players get together in a group, usually forming a circle, to agree on the strategy and signal for the next play.

You might be
a football fan if . . .

You know that

an **INCOMPLETION** is not the

result of the dog eating

someone's homework.

Incompletion is a forward pass that falls to the ground because the receiver fails to catch it or a pass that is dropped by a receiver or caught out of bounds.

You might be
a football fan if . . .

You know that

an **INTERCEPTION** is not a phone

call intended for someone else.

An interception is a pass caught in the air by a defender who is then allowed to run with the ball.

You might be
a football fan if . . .

You know that

KICKOFF is not a way to get

comfortable after coming home

from work.

Kickoff is the kick that puts the ball into play. Kickoffs occur at the start of the game, at the beginning of the second half, after each touchdown and after each field goal. A player kicks the ball to the opposing team from a tee at his own 40-yard line.

You might be
a football fan if . . .

You know that

the **LOCKER ROOM** is not

the lockup at the county jail.

The locker room is where the players dress, go for a pep talk at the half and return when the game is over to receive support and encouragement from their coaches, regardless of the score.

You might be
a football fan if . . .

You know that

a LOOSE BALL is not a ball

of yarn that a kitten rolls

around on the floor.

A loose ball is a ball not in possession of either team, such as during a pass, fumble or a kick.

You might be
a football fan if . . .

You know that

a **NEUTRAL ZONE** is not usually

declared in the middle of a

heated argument.

The neutral zone is the area between the two lines of scrimmage. The ball rests on the ground in this area before each play.

You might be
a football fan if . . .

You know that

an **OPEN RECEIVER** is not to be

confused with a person

looking for a handout.

An open receiver is a player who has no defender
closely covering him.

You might be
a football fan if . . .

You know that

a PLAY CLOCK is not the best one

to use when teaching a child

to tell time.

The play clock is the one displayed above each end zone that limits the time between plays to 40 seconds. The ball must be snapped before the clock runs down to zero.

You might be
a football fan if . . .

You know that

a **POCKET** is not where little boys
hide their treasures such as
frogs and garden snakes.

A pocket is the protection formed by other players around
the quarterback when he is throwing a pass.

You might be
a football fan if . . .

You know that

a **PUNT** is not a boat that

is propelled with a pole.

A punt is a ball kicked to the opponent by propelling
the ball with the foot. This usually is the method
of exchanging possession of the ball on the fourth down.

You might be
a football fan if . . .

You know that

a **QUARTERBACK SNEAK**

doesn't happen when a kid

sneaks a quarter from his

piggy bank.

The quarterback sneak occurs when the quarterback takes the snap from the center, keeps the ball and runs directly behind the center, who is blocking straight ahead, with the hope of gaining a small amount of yardage.

You might be
a football fan if . . .

You know that

RECOVERY is not a room at the

local hospital.

Recovery is gaining possession of a live ball after it strikes the ground.

You might be
a football fan if . . .

You know that

a RETURN is not how to get rid of

an undesired purchase.

A return occurs when a player catches the ball after a punt or kickoff and runs with it back toward the goal line.

You might be
a football fan if . . .

You know that

SCRIMMAGE is not a struggle

two neighbors might have

over an item

at a yard sale.

Scrimmage is the play that takes place when the two teams are lined up and the ball is snapped.

You might be
a football fan if . . .

You know that

SNAP is not something to do

to get attention or to mark

the beat.

The snap occurs when the center starts each down by handing or throwing the ball between his legs to a player, usually the quarterback. The snap takes place at the line of scrimmage and is also called centering the ball.

You might be
a football fan if . . .

You know that

SPECIAL TEAMS are not

related to the Olympic games.

Special teams are the players assigned to kicking plays either when their team is receiving or kicking.

You might be
a football fan if . . .

You know that

TACKLE is not what a sportsman

uses to catch a fish.

Tackle is what a defensive player does when he uses his hands and arms to bring down an offensive player who has the ball. A tackle is one of two offensive players positioned on either side of the center outside the guards but inside the ends. There are also two defensive tackles.

You might be
a football fan if . . .

You know that

a **TOUCHBACK** is not what happens

after being tagged in a race.

A touchback refers to a ball that is downed in the end zone by the receiving team following a kickoff, punt, interception or fumble recovery. The team that downed the ball gets possession of it at its 20-yard line.

SCORING

Plays that help win the game

YOU MIGHT BE A FOOTBALL FAN IF . . .

Touchdown	6
Field Goal	3
Safety	2
2 PT Conversion	2
Extra Point	1

You might be
a football fan if . . .

You know that
an **EXTRA POINT** is not an
award that preferred customers
earn at their supermarket.

The kick for one extra point may be tried from within the 10-yard line. However, a team may choose to try a 2-point conversion, which consists of one offensive play from the 3-yard line. In this case, if the ball carrier carries the ball across the goal line, his team scores two points.

You might be
a football fan if . . .

You know that
FIELD GOAL is not the posts
and crossbar at each end
of the football field.

A kick for a field goal can be made from anywhere on the field but usually is attempted within 40 yards from the goalpost. If successful, it is worth three points.

You might be
a football fan if . . .

You know that

a **SAFETY** is not a pin used

to hold a torn shirt together.

A safety occurs if an offensive ball carrier is tackled inside his own end zone. The defensive team is awarded two points, and the offensive team must take a free kick and give possession to the defense.

You might be
a football fan if . . .

You know that

a **TOUCHDOWN** is not what

happens when a plane lands

at an airport.

A touchdown, worth six points, is scored when a player carries the ball across the goal line or receives a pass in the end zone of the opposing team.

You might be
a football fan if . . .

You know that

a **TWO-POINT CONVERSION**

is not a kind of

religious experience.

After the touchdown is scored, the team can kick for an extra point or try for two points. The team must move the ball forward 3 yards into the end zone by having a player carry the ball over or having the quarterback throw the ball to the player in the end zone.

PENALTIES

Mistakes that can lose the game

You might be
a football fan if . . .

You know that

BACKFIELD IN MOTION is not

a song or a move made while

on the dance floor.

The backfield includes the offensive players—the running backs and the quarterback—who line up behind the line of scrimmage. If one of them moves toward the line before the ball is snapped, this results in a 5-yard penalty.

You might be
a football fan if . . .

You know that

CLIPPING is not something

to do with store coupons.

Clipping is an illegal blocking of an opponent below the waist from behind. This is a personal foul and is punishable by a 15-yard penalty.

You might be
a football fan if . . .

You know that

DELAY OF GAME is not called when

a child runs across the field

to go to the bathroom

or to get a hotdog.

Delay of game is any failure by a team to be ready for play within the specified time limit of any action that prolongs the game. This results in a 5-yard penalty.

You might be
a football fan if . . .

You know that

ENCROACHMENT is not what happens

when an uninvited guest

shows up for dinner.

Encroachment is the defensive penalty called when a player enters the neutral zone between the offensive and defensive lines before the ball is snapped.

You might be
a football fan if . . .

You know that

a **FACE MASK** is not a

treatment to get rid of wrinkles.

A player may not grab another player's face mask—the cage-like front of the helmet—any time during the game. The result is a 15-yard penalty.

You might be
a football fan if . . .

You know that
a **FOUL** is not related to
a Canadian goose.

A foul is any violation of football's rules by a player or a team and is punishable by a penalty. The severity of the penalty depends upon the violation.

You might be
a football fan if . . .

You know that

HOLDING is not the public display

of affection often seen

at a movie theater.

Holding is the illegal use of the hands and takes place when a player impedes the movement of an opponent by grasping any part of his body or uniform. A foul is called resulting in a penalty of 10 yards.

You might be a football fan if . . .

You know that

INTENTIONAL GROUNDING is

not the punishment a teenager

receives for breaking

curfew.

Intentional grounding may be called when a quarter-back who, as he is about to be tackled, throws the ball into an area where no eligible receiver is near enough to catch it. If the official determines that there was no chance of the pass being completed, the penalty is 15 yards and loss of down.

You might be
a football fan if . . .

You know that

OFFSIDES is not called when

ice cream drips down the cone.

An offsides penalty of 5 yards is called when any part of a player's body is in the neutral zone between the offensive and defensive line before the ball is snapped.

You might be
a football fan if . . .

You know that

PASS INTERFERENCE is not the

same as listening in on

someone's telephone call.

Pass interference is impeding an offensive or defensive player who is trying to catch a pass.

You might be
a football fan if . . .

You know that

a PERSONAL FOUL is not a pet

macaw, parakeet or

other exotic bird.

A personal foul is called on a player for any unsportsmanlike conduct toward the officials, players or coaches. A 15-yard penalty is imposed. The infraction can result in the removal of the player from the game.

OFFICIAL FOOTBALL SIGNALS
HIGH SCHOOL AND COLLEGE

1 — Ball ready for play / *Untimed down

2 — Start clock

3 — Time-out / Discretionary or injury time-out (follow by tapping hands on chest)

4 — TV/Radio time-out

5 — Touchdown / Field goal / Point(s) after touchdown

6 — Safety

7 — Ball dead / Touchback (move side to side)

8 — First down

9 — Loss of down

10 — Incomplete forward pass / Penalty declined / No play, no score / Toss option delayed

11 — Legal touching of forward pass or scrimmage kick

12 — Inadvertent whistle (Face Press Box)

13 — Disregard flag

161

OFFICIAL FOOTBALL SIGNALS
HIGH SCHOOL AND COLLEGE

14 End of period

15 Sideline warning

16 First touching Illegal touching (NCAA)

17 Uncatchable Forward Pass (NCAA)

18 Encroachment (NF) Offside Defense (NCAA)

19 Illegal procedure False start Illegal formation Encroachment Offense (NCAA)

20 Illegal shift - 2 hands Illegal motion - 1 hand

21 Delay of game

22 Substitution infraction

23	24	27	28
Failure to wear required equipment	Illegal helmet contact	Unsportsmanlike conduct Noncontact foul	Illegal participation

29	30	31	32	33
Sideline interference	Running into (NCAA) or Roughing Kicker or Holder	Illegal batting Illegal kicking (Followed by pointing toward toe for kicking)	Invalid fair catch signal (NF) Illegal fair catch signal	Forward pass interference Kick catching interference

34	35	36	37	38
Roughing passer	Illegal pass Illegal forward handing	Intentional grounding	Ineligible downfield on pass	Personal foul

163

OFFICIAL FOOTBALL SIGNALS
HIGH SCHOOL AND COLLEGE

39 Clipping

40 Blocking below waist / Illegal block

41 Chop block

42 Holding/obstructing / Illegal use of hands/arms (NCAA)

43 Illegal use of hands or arms (NF) / Illegal block in the back (NCAA)

44 Helping runner / Interlocked blocking

45 Grasping face mask or helmet opening

46 Tripping

47 Player disqualification

Index of Terms

About the Authors

Dorothy France, along with her late husband Carl, has been an avid sports enthusiast since the late 1950s when she taught high school. Career changes led her into the fields of world hunger relief and refugee affairs. She is a retired teacher and minister and author of six books.

Her grandsons, Jason and David Frankle, have a love for football that began when they played youth football in kindergarten. Jason, a 1999 graduate of Copley (OH) High School, played quarterback, linebacker and holder positions for the football team. He coached youth basketball and was statistician for the baseball team. He currently plays quarterback at Muskingum College, New Concord, OH.

David, a member of the Class of 2001 at Copley, plays wide receiver, defensive back and special teams positions on the football team. He is also a member of the wrestling team and uses skills from his earlier gymnastics training for both sports.

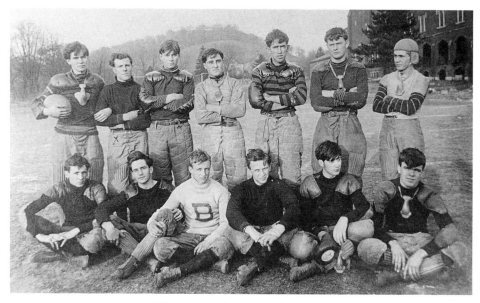

Wearers of the "B" - 1905
Bethany College, Bethany, West Virginia
Alma mater of author Dorothy France
Photo courtesy R. Jeanne Cobb, Bethany College Archives

Notes

Autographs of Favorite Players

Autographs of Favorite Players